The Three Pigs

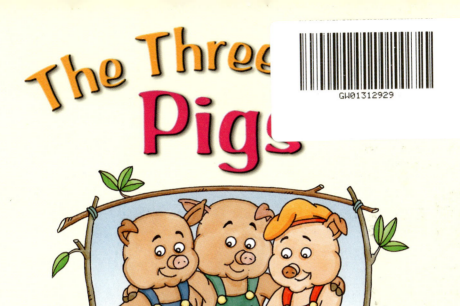

Contents

The Three Little Pigs
A traditional tale — 2

Where's Wolf?
A poem — 21

Before or After?
Picture stories to tell — 22

Animal Homes
A report — 24

The House of Straw
Rules and a letter — 26

The Wolf's Tail
The wolf's point of view — 28

Think and Link
Questions to discuss — 30

Once upon a time,
there were three little pigs.
They lived with their mother
in a house in the woods.

One day Mother Pig said, "It's time for you to build houses of your own."

So the three little pigs packed their things and set off.

Soon the first little pig found some straw.

"I will build my house of straw," he said – and he did!

A little way along, the second little pig found some sticks.

"I will build my house of sticks," he said – and he did!

The third little pig had
a different plan.

"I don't want just straw or sticks.
I will build my house of bricks,"
he said.

He found what he needed,
and he began to work.

Someone was watching the three little pigs. It was a big, bad, hungry wolf.

First the wolf went to the house of straw. "Little pig, little pig, let me in," he called.

"No!" cried the pig.
"I will not let you in,
not by the hair
of my chinny chin chin!"

"Then I'll huff, and I'll puff,
and I'll blow your house down!"
snarled the wolf – and he DID!

The first little pig ran
as fast as he could
to the house of sticks.

Soon the wolf was at the door.
"Little pigs, little pigs,
let me in!" he called.

"No!" cried the pigs.
"We will not let you in,
not by the hair
of our chinny chin chins!"

"Then I'll huff, and I'll puff,
and I'll blow your house down!"
yelled the wolf – and he DID!

The pigs raced to the house of bricks. Just as they slammed the door, they heard the wolf outside.

"Little pigs, little pigs, LET ME IN!"

"No!" cried the pigs.
"We will not let you in,
not by the hair
of our chinny chin chins!"

"Then I'll huff, and I'll puff,
and I'll blow your house down!"
roared the wolf.

The wolf huffed, and he puffed, but he could not blow the house down.

So he climbed up onto the roof and into the chimney.

"Ouch!" cried the wolf, as the flame touched the tip of his tail. He shot back up the chimney in fright.

The big bad wolf jumped off the roof and ran away. He never came back – and the three little pigs lived happily ever after.

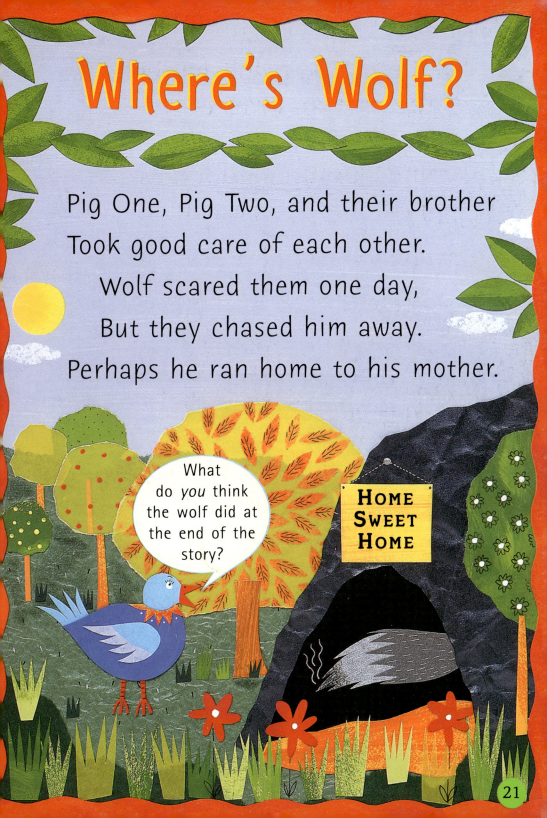

Before or After?

Talk about each picture, and the scene it shows. Could it come before or after the story you know?

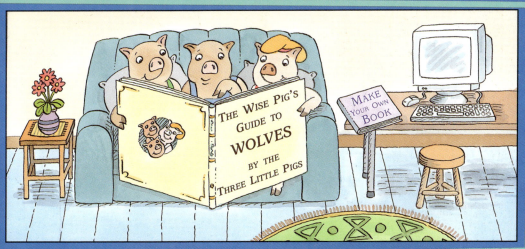

Read about some creatures whose homes have different features.

Animal Homes

Some animals make homes for themselves or their babies. They make their homes from things they find around them.

Match the creatures on this page to the homes in the circles.

Weaver bird

Beaver

Termites

Beavers make lodges from sticks.

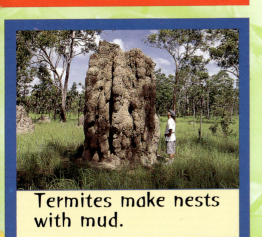

Termites make nests with mud.

Weaver birds make nests with grass.

Some ants make nests with living leaves. They use sticky silk to stick the leaves together.

Some wasps make paper nests for baby wasps. They chew up wood or leaves to make the paper.

What other animals make homes?

25

The pig is ready with his straw and tools. How well does his plan match the building rules?

The House of Straw

CUCKOO COUNTY BUILDING RULES

Safety First!

Cuckoo County has safety rules that you must follow if you are building a house.

You may build your house only with:
- wood
- brick
- stone

Before you build, you must send the plans for your new house to Cuckoo County.

Dear Cuckoo County,

Did you know you forgot to put straw on your list of things to build with? Here is a drawing of the house I am planning to build with straw. I'm sure you'll agree that it will be a very nice, very safe house!

Best wishes,
Littlus Pig

Now, if the wolf could have his say, what might *he* tell us about that day?

The Wolf's Tail

Last week, I tried to make friends with some pigs. I saw a pig building a very pretty house made of straw, and I went to say hello. Then my nose began to tickle, as it often does in the spring. So I blew my nose hard, as Mother taught me. Just then, the straw house collapsed! The wind must have blown it over!

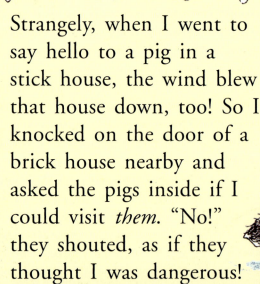

Strangely, when I went to say hello to a pig in a stick house, the wind blew that house down, too! So I knocked on the door of a brick house nearby and asked the pigs inside if I could visit *them*. "No!" they shouted, as if they thought I was dangerous!

Then I remembered what Mother always says: *"If at first you don't succeed, try, try, try again."* I knew they would like me if they met me. So I climbed down the chimney of the brick house to surprise them!

But the pigs did something very silly. They built a fire, and I burned my tail. Don't they know that you shouldn't light a fire until you've checked the chimney for visitors? I will never ever try to make friends with *those* pigs again.

Think and Link

Story and Poem

Which characters or events in the poem match the story? Which are different?

Stories from Pictures

What pictures from this book give you ideas for writing? Which pictures would you most like to write about? Why?

Story and Report

How are the pigs' houses different from real animal homes? How are they the same as real animal homes?

Rules, Letter, and Story

Why do you think the little pig thinks straw is a good building material? Do you agree or disagree? Why?

Words About Wolves

Make lists of words that describe the wolf in the story, the poem, and The Wolf's Tail. What words are the same in the lists? Why?

30